LOVE IN THIN PLACES

Confessions of a Cathedral Chaplain

— DAVID GRIEVE —

Sacristy
Press

Sacristy Press
PO Box 612, Durham, DH1 9HT

www.sacristy.co.uk

First published in 2019 by Sacristy Press, Durham

Sacristy Limited, registered in England & Wales, number 7565667

British Library Cataloguing-in-Publication Data
A catalogue record for the book is available from the British Library

ISBN 978-1-78959-014-2

To the vergers, volunteers, staff, pilgrims, visitors,
saints, clergy and chaplains at Durham Cathedral,
past, present and to come, with thanks

Foreword

Like so many coming into the North East of England, Durham Cathedral has won a treasured place in David Grieve's heart since his first encounter 60 years ago, rooting him in the spirituality of the Land of the Northern Saints.

The North East in general, and Durham in particular, is a richly textured environment, full of *marauding invaders*, *journey between* and *relics*. These all find their place in David's poetry evoking not only the physical landscape of the travelling band who set off from Holy Island, Lindisfarne, but also their destination. At first a modest Saxon shrine-church where the Cloisters now stand, and then the glory of one of Europe's greatest Norman Cathedrals built to house the translated saint.

For those who know the building intimately, *Love in Thin Places* is in part an exploration of the physical space, as well as an interior journey into the soul. The Venerable Bede in the Galilee Chapel, the magnificent Cloisters, the Chapel of the Nine Altars and the Durham Light Infantry all gain a mention—as do the Deanery Chapel of the Holy Cross and even Durham LEGO Cathedral. The poems could well be used as a pilgrimage through the site, but perhaps of equal inspiration will be the spiritual and liturgical journeys these conjure up. The invocation of the Holy Spirit, the *embracing reticence* of faith, the wounded love of the Christ who shares our wounds:

So intensely sad he looks today, does Jesus.
Is he mirroring my feelings of sadness at injustices and betrayals?

The Cathedral Chaplains, of which David is a valued member, are part of the 800-strong army of volunteers who are the life-blood of Durham Cathedral and embody our rootedness within the region. Welcomers, stewards, guides, conservators, teachers, broderers—and Chaplains—these are the living descendants of the *haliwerfolc*, the Community of Cuthbert, who keep the shrine alive.

But *Love in Thin Places* is not merely a collection of poetry, however exquisite and well-fashioned. It is every bit as much a meditation and prayer; it is an invitation for the reader to join in the contemplation and to be transformed even by the words on the page:

In this holy place,
may the peace of Christ Reconciler enter every heart.

In this holy place,
may the mind of Christ Eternal Word
transform and renew us in his image.

And from this holy place,
send us out to live justly, to love mercy and to embody the Kingdom

The Very Revd Andrew Tremlett
Dean of Durham, November 2018

Preface

I first saw Durham as a small child back in the 1950s, out of a window on the London-to-Newcastle night sleeper train, a real engine, coal-fired and steaming. We spent the night in a siding somewhere near York. Mum made sure we boys were awake in time to see Durham, and then we arrived at Newcastle in time for breakfast. We were travelling up to stay with family. Once, at least, we drove up from our home in Kent; we have photos of Palace Green with our car and hardly another parked outside lecture rooms, which I would later attend myself. And we once went to a *Son et Lumière* in the Cathedral. I still remember 60 years later the awe and mystery that I felt on that visit. I didn't know then the phrase "Thin Place", but Durham Cathedral was thin to me from then on.

Durham was where I went to university, at St John's College, where I studied theology and grew in faith; where I met my wife. County Durham was where, after two curacies, we returned for my call to be Vicar of Pelton in the 1980s. It's the county in which we've lived ever since.

During an illness which led to my early retirement and changed my life entirely, I began to write poetry. In 1989 we moved to a Durham suburb called Pity

Me, and I did pity myself quite frequently, but writing and learning how to write became part of that sense of vocation which never left me. I was so blessed to be mentored by Dr Ruth Etchells, who rubbed off many of my poetic rough edges, opened my eyes to poetry making, and was a friend praying for my family.

A colleague mentioned the possibility of being a volunteer Cathedral Chaplain at Durham every so often. I got in touch with the Cathedral and soon was shadowing a seasoned chaplain. I've been doing it ever since, astounded and blessed by this God-breathed building. I still find surprises and delights almost each time I allow the building to speak to me, and have often found myself having to be still and write down. I've included many of these in this collection, which is my *Confessions* (Confessions of faith rather than misdemeanours, as we moderns often assume). This Cathedral and so many sacred spaces have ways of speaking for themselves and pointing towards God who is love. I hope to be there often in years to come, and that it will be visible somewhere in the City of God at Kingdom Come.

I am very glad to have been published again by Sacristy Press, and give my heartfelt thanks to Richard Hilton, Thomas Ball, Erik Sharman, Natalie Watson and all the team for their friendly, efficient and kind help.

David Grieve
Castle Eden, Co. Durham, November 2018

Contents

Lindisfarne, Durham and the Journey Between

You came here not to get away,
but to get back.

You came here to step aside
and see this thing that happens here,
its setting and history,
its stories and memories,
its ruins and restorations,
its dead and its living
all conveying the hope and then
the shape of glory.

The call you had
was to come and to go,
imprinted with the ebbing, flowing,
waxing, waning
hope and shape of glory,
and with Christ the beginning and ending.

You came here not to get away,
but to get back.

In Durham

In Durham I have to believe,
for a thousand years of faith,
of fear channelled,
of hope invested,
of glory alive in stone,
fill my vision at every turn of the road.

In such a setting,
mystery overshadows uncertainty,
atheism is beside the point,
and the past is a safe haven
for the future's explorations.

In the Nave in the Way

She stood there, halfway between the Saints
and told me, *I feel their energies.*

This was many years ago,
before I had been to her country,
but somehow I had already felt for myself,
before I knew it.

God's thin places are many and various,
wherever holiness makes its mark,
wherever prayer has been faithful in active love.

The past is still present
and God's holiness palpable.
It steps outdoors
in lives which, knowing their great need,
express their gratitude
in the energies of love and service.

This present will be past,
part of the thread.

Further In

As I enter the great church
my new shoes click
loudly on the flagstones,
so I slow my pace.

But this only reminds me
of school prefects
on dorm duty after lights out,
scarily parading power
on bare, squeaky floorboards.

I think of Frank,
who I first met here at The Crossing,
dressed as I am now for service,
who has just begun to rest.
   Light eternal . . .

Visitors crowd round the shrine,
and in the buzz
of conversations and questions,
there are reports
both of simplicity and mystery,
of something that is as it has been here.

Private prayer and an upwards glance
bring into focus
God's recent and present touch.

Here is a backbone,
not a cage for faith,
but a place for the heart to fly.

The Dying of the Saint

Take me with you if ever you leave, Herefrith.

Shall you be lonely, Father, if we go?
There are many others,
who await the Resurrection on Lindisfarne.

I am part of you all, and you of me, my Child.
You must not keep me apart from you,
because God wills it so.

It shall be done, Father,
if ever God calls us away.
But you mustn't think of that now.
Perhaps the Lord will grant you to us for many years yet.

He has told me, my Child, that I am to die soon.

Then, Father, please take the herbs that will help you.
Your children grieve that you are in such pain.

I will not.
It is enough to chant my Lord's praise
with a clear head. Think
of his dreadful pain on the cross.
I will imitate him in bearing it.
All I want is his holy body and blood.

Father, I will make preparations.

And is the boat ready, my Child?

Holy Island to Durham

With a grandmother,
a mother and a shepherd boy in mind
we journeyed across sands of time.

We were not fleeing.
No marauding invaders,
swords or axes in hand,
were at our backs
to displace us,
to remove us from the City of God
and turn us into nomads.

But we were urgent.
The sea that had drawn back,
unrelenting in its return,
pressed home that we came in order to go back,
that we are called not to remain cut off from the main,
but to embrace again the dispersed calling,
to take to heart the Dismissal at Eucharist's end.

We braved light-heartedly the Pilgrims' Way,
whose mudflats suck and grip as tenaciously as sin.
We laughed in the face of tumbles
and the stains of 'Cuddy's mud'.

And we were serious,
signposted by Cuthbert,
he who as shepherd boy
had once been star-struck towards Christ.

And journey's end was another beginning,
when the great Church resounded
with high thanksgiving and the joy of association.

We, Cuthbert's people, hearing again the great stories told,
are among those whom Christ has honoured
    with the cry of his voice:

Wherever I lead you, follow.

Glory and Heartache

At the crib in Durham Mary keeps vigil.
In complete stillness, while the child is asleep,
she sits at a distance taking it all in, this birth,
but her back, bending towards him, has a mother's longings.

There is more potency in this wooden portrayal:
Joseph is standing further back, hero in the shadows
and proud in tender care of his family.

His tool bag is at his feet.
Perhaps, in the rush, he made that stool.
It is well made.

The shepherds attend;
one is kneeling in wonder, in worship;
one stands erect in the nobility
conferred by the Christ-child
on all who will receive him.

Glory is palpable.

The kings and their treasures are yet to arrive as I watch.
They will be needed in Haiti
for a prolonged Epiphany.
The sword that will pierce Mary
is at work there too.
All the impulses of incarnate love,
mediated in compassionate human action,
cry that there must,
there will be recovery,
and the shouts of the poor will be heard.

Word in Our Hearing

O Word eternally spoken,
now a baby awoken,
born a helpless stranger,
inhabits a poor manger.

Grant us who hear the story
to wonder at your glory
wrapped in human frailty,
disclosing to us deity.

O Word who spoke, creating,
and Love forever inviting,
grant us who hear the story
to enter into glory.

Jesus Baptised

The sun of righteousness bathes in Jordan.
The fire is immersed in water.
God our king made holy by man.
Strange and mysterious new order.

Riches to rags make known all glory.
Living is granted through drowning.
This point in time tells a timeless story.
His emptying of self is our crowning.

Faith

Faith, embracing reticence,
glad to speak when words are called for,
ready for silence, for adoration.

Faith, discipling enthusiasm
into channelled eagerness,
a closet love seeking his attention most.

Faith, marked by obedience,
wanting to be a reflection and not a distraction.
Heady with heaven's early gifts,
heading for Home.

Nine Altars Prayer

I see at altar and in prayer,
icon, frontal, everywhere,
Glory, Holiness, Life.

In coloured glass and painted art,
in Love's immediacy and dart,
Glory, Holiness, Life.

In pilgrim, tourist and in staff,
in cry of pain or happy laugh,
Glory, Holiness, Life.

In all God's mediated goodness
outweighing human foolishness,
Glory, Holiness, Life.

At the Water's Edge

At the water's edge Godric used to walk and then wade
out to the deep.

Today's tourists amble around hand in hand.
Children chase each other in and out of the Priory ruins
stumbling in their innocence over the cross
    which marks the saint's grave,
a madding crowd which,
had he met in life,
would have made him seek a still more distant solitude.

Bank holiday visitors disperse quietly
    across the bridge over the Wear
and run their young and their dogs along the
opposite bank.

The sun, weakly, catches the river's flow in its fading
    light while the farmer's stern *Keep Out* notice
cannot prevent the evening mist's rapid progress.

Hermits die and visitors go, but, day in and day out,
Wear flows through Finchale,
an eloquent witness to the eternal in time
whose words with mankind leave
their mark here as everywhere.

Prayer in a Thin Place

In this holy place,
may glory in fullness displace self-absorption.

In this holy place,
may the energy of deposited faith refresh every soul.

In this holy place,
may the light of Christ Ever Shining drive all darkness away.

In this holy place,
may the peace of Christ Reconciler enter every heart.

In this holy place,
may the mind of Christ Eternal Word
transform and renew us in his image.

And from this holy place,
send us out to live justly, to love mercy
    and to embody the Kingdom.

Ash Wednesday

Rub it in, God,
the ashes on my forehead,
the oil on my hair, my body, my soul.

Is there enough world-weariness yet,
terror on all sides,
self-defence mechanisms kicking us into fear?

Rub it in, God,
the ashes on my forehead,
the oil on my hair, my body, my soul.

Selfishness begins at home.
Please do not disturb.
I can't cope with your Kingdom
kicking my door in.

Rub it in, God,
the ashes on my forehead,
the oil on my hair, my body, my soul.

So it is Lent

It begins for me not with a mark on the forehead,
but the sight of dawn breaking,
God's visual aid teaching that newness comes from the breaking,
as for Adam, for Jacob, for Ruth, for Jesus, for Saul, it did,
as it has done for so many, Stephen, Valentine, Alban, Oswald,
and the countless we cannot begin to name.

There is much to break, even though it
    has all already been broken
through the lightning strike of Calvary.
There remains, for each generation, a command to obey
and an example to follow from the Broken Man.

There remains the easy pathway which demands no struggle,
and the too-complicated struggle that confuses the pathway.
There is still the freshness of the Ash Wednesday frankness.
We remain dust. We are invited to have our starlight rekindled.

When It Comes Down to It

Duty must,
Self will,
Love may.

At the North Quire Aisle Crucifix

Christ of the bent agonised back,
dying and misshapen for love's sake,
be known in all the world's contortions,
in its *La'ma Sabachthani*,
and be the air it gasps for.

O world so frightened by its own powers,
so fearful of unfettered energies,
know that you are known and
held in God's weakness.
What he promised he will fulfil.

On Being Drawn In

If you stand and look at the Transfiguration Window,
you will see all sorts and needs,
and people around its fringes,
and the Proper Man at its heart,
with Peter, James and John.
Peggy too, I dare say, and Bella and Mary.

In fact there in the blaze of light are countless others,
and more yet to be, but we see them in Jesus.

And as you walk on, Jesus is seen in you.

On St Hild's Day

At prayer, I open faith's calendar
and see St Hild in her shining,
jewel of the Church whose yearning
for the Gospel united the divided,
and with her the surrounding cloud,
for Glory breaches the dividing walls
and reaches even into the soul,
if even for that one moment that is sufficient,
strengthening the desire not to possess it,
but to follow its leading, out into the task of healing.

Both abroad and here, at home,
the call is to find that single eye,
the clear sight that accepts all as equally loved,
valued and united in Christ's only body,
he who is End as he is Beginning,
Lord of Glory.

Be In No Hurry to Pray

Be in no hurry to pray.
Wait till your body and mind
navigate to your soul's anchor.

There may be nothing or much to say,
plenty to hear, a barrier to unblock.

Lamenting or praising
in litany or impromptu cry,
you have prayed before you began.

God is near, and in weakness we attune.
Christ is the attunement made long before.

Drawing Closer, Please

Like dry timber flame-leaping high,
let my heart be.

Like a hot lover, elating a cry,
let my soul be.

Like a bird swift-soaring from earth to sky,
let my mind be.

Like a tough soldier, ready to die,
let my strength be.

As empty hands grasping what others release,
let mine, letting go, discover your peace.

Prayer after the Venerable Bede

Let me drink in with delight, good Jesus,
I implore you,
    the worship that I am here to offer,
    the service that I am here to perform,
    the beauty that I see
        in faces expressing wonder,
        in objects expressing truth.

And through all the words of your knowledge,
    spoken and read,
    chiselled and carved,
    painted and depicted,
        will you bless and strengthen me
        to live for your praise and glory?

Prayer on a Dark Day

Dark earliness on a three-candle morning
as the swirl of incense wafts in front of God's face.
He saw that all that he had made was good, and he rested.

I suddenly remember that today is 9/11.
The clammy cold darkness less opaque than God's mystery,
a despoiling cloud of hate and death rolling across the world
which chokes and flails around in grief and rage,
a volcano erupting still,
a quake whose aftershocks still endanger.

The prayer of mere helplessness
at an icon of the broken Man
is an accepted offering,
rising like smoke through a chimney
but piercing the clouds beyond our knowledge.

The Chapel of the Holy Cross

You enter this place simply,
bowing your head,
for Eucharist,
for quiet,
for security and protection
in the dark, dangerous night.

It is uncluttered, plain, simple.
You might use a 'holding cross' as you pray
("Simply to thy cross I cling"),
or be aware of echoes of shame
at costing God his life.

Cold as the grave such a place can be.

But light rises in the East,
the ever-wounded, ever-living Lord,
and you can turn your eyes upon him,
you his remodelled, living stones,
his holy people,
bearers of the Holy Cross.

On This Particular Day

I saw such grief.
I heard of such a sadness and loss.
I was told of such betrayal of faith but a desire to move on.
I met such happiness;
a couple on their first date, here within these walls;
another drawn here by Cuthbert and
    Godric and full of questions.

All these emotions mirrored in my own.

And I saw beauty in tears,
in the prayer of letting a loved one go,
in the candle lit for words which could not be unspoken.
I saw the quiet, steady flow of young and old
attracted by something they cannot express,
for he surpasses our understanding.

All these have been here today, and he has touched them,
he who is, here.

Meri Dies

If you were in the North Cloister,
it might catch your eyes, particularly on a sunny day;
Meri Dies, chiselled into a flagstone.

It once caught the imagination of a visitor who rushed to ask me,
Is this where Mary is buried?

If only!

Imagination is often more enlightening
than stone-cold fact,
though sadly not here.

I think of the monks toiling at their manuscripts
and glancing at their sundial
to see how long till their midday break,
but I don't have all the facts.

But sunshine streams in here on us, as it did on them,
and my flitting mind lets imagination lift off:

All the truth tellers and recorders of glory,
the dealers in discovery and exploration,
the describers of longitude and latitude
and all who find out the mysteries of starry sky or tiniest cell,
each one within the compass of God's knowledge,
all represented here in Meri Dies.

I was here in the middle of the day,
and I saw that it was good.

Congregation

(= Graduation at Durham University)

A cascade of applause interrupts my praying.
Cloudbursts punctuate today's last words,
but rejoicing deafens the thunder.
The Cathedral is a stage set for rewards.

For my assignment I have taken up a station
in the Shrine of St Cuthbert.
May I serve as he did, is my prayer.
He is almost visible,
his presence tangible,
his influence pervasive in the teamwork of welcome here.

It is Jesus to whom we all point.
Our *Ecce Homo* is gentle but not faint nor lacklustre.
In this sacred space alive with glory,
host to a multitude of celebrations,
I am refreshed, as are so many,
by a stream of *Glorias* cascading through eternity.

He is here.

The Durham Light Infantry Chapel

Standards, hanging proudly, faded and worn
in this church built through war,
tell us,
speak your memories to our children.

Remembrance Books, Cross of the Trenches,
wreaths and Rolls of Honour,
all that rouses the memory,

shout of the soldiers and their sacrifice,
their sweet sacrifice it was said,
dying for their country in the killing fields.

And stir us to answer
the Master's call
daily to lay down our lives.

My National Poetry Day Poem

Could I do it in a day,
I would build Durham Cathedral,
poem in stone,
voice of a thousand years,
anthem of all the unknown years,
since Adam knew he was awake
and Eve knew she could talk.

It is, of course, already made,
and in the making,
project of one and countless poets,
bearing the scars of brutal editing
but singing the Gospel song
of seductive, mysterious God.

So I gave up,
and wrote this poem instead.

Cuthbert's Day

20th March

In your day, unencumbered, you kept your gaze on eternity,
so that you could look on life and see glory.

Your voice was heard telling the praise
of the intervening, incarnating, embracing power
that stretched love to no limits.

In your day, you led in your doing
and were transparent in your bearing.
You wrote no book but were yourself the illustration
from which Christ leapt from the page.

You loved all that you saw in your day,
even as, having looked widely,
you put it all into the upward gaze.

Today
on your day
we honour the presence that continues to bless.

Glory on the Mountain

And he was transfigured before them.
Matthew 17:2

Brighter than the lightning across the sky
that gainsaid the darkness when he died.
For when he gave his victory cry,
all heaven flashed and angels cried
Gloria in Excelsis!

Prefigured when the saints appeared,
Moses and Elijah who spoke with him.
His eternal glory by angels revered,
revealed to those who followed him.
Gloria in Excelsis!

His tomb discarded, their room invaded,
he showed his glory in body and breath.
Eternal, once contracted, now expanded,
God himself has overcome death.
Gloria in Excelsis!

Now You Know. You Heard It from Me

I am writing, Mrs Davidson,
(may I call you Mary?),
as your late son's bereaved friend.
I want to tell you more than "Killed in Action",
so that you know. You heard it from me.

He was one of Our Heroes, our "lions led by donkeys",
though in fact he was a coward, Mary. We all were.
He puked and choked, he wet and shat,
and when he was hit, he bled and went to pieces, many pieces,
just like they all did.
He was just like the next man.
Now you know. You heard it from me.

He died very quickly. There wasn't much to keep him living.
And they did what they could with the remains.
Now you know. You heard it from me.

I wasn't there, Mary. I had to run an errand back behind the lines.
Just as well there's someone to tell you.
We're not all meant to die like him,
God knows.

On Being Inquisitive, Acquisitive, Agnostic and Faithful

Did we imagine it all about Jesus?
Oh I hope so, I really do hope so.
To have done otherwise would be misery.
To have spurned the Spirit's invitation to let
the Gospel sear our hearts and minds
with the life-giving fire of entering into his story
and making it ours as well,
it might as well have been history. We should have stayed
in Sunday School.

There is a greed in us that is pure good;
that insatiable desire to know him who now knows us,
to follow his scent and spot the trail that he has laid,
planting our footsteps where he has trod;
that picking up messages that he left,
hoping that we would;
the unravelling of something, at least,
of the enigmatic, mysterious pathway towards fullness when,
at last,
we who consume and acquire
are face to face with God.

Agnosticism is the key to understanding here;
knowing that we learn through metaphor and simile,
and that certainty is as solid as vapour.
What we know is that we do not know fully;
provisionally, we stake our lives
on what he has provided;
putting weight on the step out into the unseen,
faith is supported and carried,
and we are not disappointed.

So we go on searching, because he has searched for us,
and until Kingdom come that is our forward direction.

I Think

I am shaped by place and person,
by beginnings and continuings
and the scouring of a future wind
which is already hard.

I am adapted and changing,
still the same and seeking stillness
on a rotating planet and in a
never-the-same environment.

I am fed with pills and chemicals,
fed up with blandness,
nourished by sacramental, audible, edible,
consumable and visual gift.

I am yet to understand,
seeking to serve,
dying to please,
happy to know.

I anticipate resurrection,
fear self's destruction,
contemplate absorption,
wonder at completion.

Psalm for Today

You know, O GOD,
that just because I believe strongly
doesn't mean I hurt mildly,

just because I move away from trauma
doesn't mean I'm not still raw,

just because my surface is calm
doesn't mean there is no deep turmoil,

just because I can fail to be honest
doesn't mean I cannot realise a problem.

God be praised
for allowing the past to be present, the long ago to be now.

God be praised
in the depths, the hidden and revealed,
the unhappy and disabling,
the nasty and destructive.

Lord of it all,
let me shelter under the shadow of your wings.
Let us ride out the storms together,
the hurricanes of memory and those to come.
Lead me in the way of righteousness,
however dark the valley, enjoying the table,
looking ahead to fullness.

God

God is patient all of the time,
but is no doormat that doesn't see
the dirt done in his name.
All of the time God is kind.

God is kind all of the time,
but not the kind that pretends
not to notice the abuse of love.
All of the time God is truthful.

God is truthful all of the time,
but does not trumpet the wrongs of others,
preferring to endure.
All of the time God is there.

God is there all of the time,
but not in a way that cramps
our freedom to do without him.
All of the time God is good.

God is good all of the time,
but not merely because
we experience his great goodness.
All of the time God is.

God is, all of the time.
God just is.

Oned

What might be if we were Oned?
United, as we would say,
but at a greater depth than being a season
    ticket holder in a football club,
or a shareholder in some conglomerate.

If, as God is, we could be one, Oned, perfectly
united in person and purpose and in every way,
inhabiting, motivated by and moving in the love
that has always been love and has always been loving,
then what might be not happening,
and what might be done to heal this creation,
torn apart by Adam's and Eve's dysfunctional children?

After all, if all were Oned there'd have been no widening fracture
of original wholeness, from the first excuse to the
    repeated slaughters of the innocent.
No exploitation of the poor, for none would be poor
and none would be rich. All would be one. Oned with God.

Ah, you say, do not deny us our diversity, our
    differences, our hard-won, deserved wellbeing.
I won't.

But all shall not be well until we are Oned.

Glad to Be Here

Tears surprise me in the Feretory as,
kneeling before St Cuthbert, they well up
and demand attention.
I have prayed pilgrim prayers,
prayers that Christians love to pray
and the one the Saviour taught.

Pastors cry as well as comfort,
and I have brought myself as I am to Christ this morning.
I have entrusted to him once again those on my heart.
I thought I was calm,
but tears taught me to be myself,
not in control but guided by him whom I serve
and love and worship.

There in the Feretory I had had such intimacy,
a closeness which enables and motivates me.
I am glad to be here.

An Active Memory

Cuthbert, your attractive presence
is another of the mysteries here;
you are an active memory,
as are Bede and Oswald.

The energy of your life, its imprint on our hearts,
the prayers to God generated here
over so many changing times,
amount to talkative holiness, a felt holiness
in this Church where God discloses himself so variously.

As it was for you there then, we make Eucharist here.
We journey on with Scripture to speak to us,
Psalms and hymns to give us voice,
interceding through Christ and offering apostolic ministry,
as you did.

You, once the keeper of sheep,
are still gathering a flock for Christ.
God grant that we be faithful, like you,
and welcome all as he draws them closer.

Relics

A holiness imprinted
within sacred space cannot be erased
merely by smashing a shrine.

Nor with the passing years
has God taken back what he gave.

The likeness once earthed
in shepherd and saint
continues to matter,
to speak of and
give shape to faith.

Here,
where prayer, love,
enquiry and knowledge
all persist,
looking not so much to
antiquity as to eternity
for the wellsprings of life,

St Cuthbert's power
to bless for Christ
stirs me afresh
in this many-sainted,
increasingly new place.

A shadow of his future self,
his waves ripple quietly outwards
as they will, until Christ,
depicted over the saint's tomb,
fills the earth with his glory.

One Day It Will Cover the Mountains

Listen to the silence
of holiness, prayer and love for God
leaching out of the very stones.

Touch, join the flowing faith-stream here,
springing out of God, river head and source.

Holiness, faith, adhering despite the necessary noise
of rehearsals and announcements.

The new Dean, announced today
for the next raft of time carried by this stream,
will play a part, just a part, but his part
in the flow of which there can be no stopping,
for if you were to dam it up and arrest it,
    it would burst out elsewhere.

One day it will cover the mountains.

Back Here Again

My heart stirred, is stirring now.
I had been elsewhere, marvelling at Cotswold stone colleges,
fine churches, and exquisite villages with thatched cottages,
and I was blessed.

Then I came back here.
I saw it on my journey in, standing in majesty.
Through the traffic I drove, and turned up the Bailey,
and my heart stirred with home-coming joy.

This, for me, is a Thin Place, ever moving.
The veil shifts as the wind blows it,
and I am differently blessed each time I visit.
For God, in his building and in his people,
is always speaking, always disclosing, always touching.

There is endless space in a Thin Place.
That is the paradox of mystery,
and the encounter with what is beyond our grasp
denies that faith can be reduced
to mere culture or dismissed as fable.

Lego Cathedral

Brick by brick and patiently,
laid-down love of majesty,
the model describes a shape,
and the shape points beyond.

Week by week and gradually,
as time once carved eternity,
the model describes a life,
and the life points beyond.

Step by step excitedly,
completion speaks of momentary,
and the model describes an outline,
and the outline points beyond.

Coming and Going With God

It's so loud! So exciting!
Here are the school leavers, come to thank God
for all they have learnt, for all their friends,
and to trust him.

The past is so great. The future's a bit scary.
They will be going up to Big School.

Each year the groups come in turn,
the families so proud,
Mums wondering at how quickly
the years have gone.

So different to many Cathedral services.
Shouts and screams of joy agree with
the Archdeacon's "How great is this place!"
Other visitors are slightly bemused:
"I wasn't expecting this."

Cathedrals are made of stone and elastic.
They curve in and out of time and eternity,
mystery and matter.
The same energy flows through it all.

Saying It Again

Reflections on Fenwick Lawson's
Pieta in Durham Cathedral

(*previously published in* Hope in Dark Places)

Saying it, as at the beginning,

now at the ending,

at the foot of the cross,

he, taken down lifeless Son of God,

her son,

first born, child of such promise. Contorted

He lies there,

all breath extracted,

and hardly a breath in her,

rooted in the rock hardness of grief.

Dropped hands are open,

unclenched,

in the let it be position

of helpless love's letting go.

Eyes numbed shut,
she does not see how,
in *rigor mortis*,
a distended arm sticks up as if
to grasp her by the hand.

It is too early for her to believe,
but soon he will overturn
such relentless certainty
and invite her into the
let it be
of resurrection.

Peace and Justice

So intensely sad he looks today, does Jesus.
Is he mirroring my feelings of sadness at injustices and betrayals;
the young girls mutilated by FGM, and
those forced into prostitution and modern slavery?
Is he upset for the disabled people unjustly
    treated by State, society and Church?
Is it the environment in danger, the loss of animal
    life, or the slaughter of any innocents?

But he who bleeds for creation has no
    more blood to give, or water.
This Jesus is dead. I saw him at the Pieta,
a laid aside, broken corpse,
all spent and empty, no use at all now.

Yet, I cannot linger in sadness,
not while I can still pray,
not while he lives, as he does now,
not while the Spirit whom the Saviour sent
agitates into love and action
the whole responding circle of humans,
whether or not they call him Lord.

I say Glory to God who so loves.

In a While

It takes a while for the eyes to adjust
to the brightness of Resurrection,
for the mind and the leaping heart
to process what cannot be so but is so.

It takes a while to realise that
our cheering, our applause, our joy
are not for the *status quo ante* being restored.

It takes a while to grasp that we cannot
contain him, limit him, pin him down
or keep him from trailblazing
on the far side of the dark glass.

In a while, at Kingdom come,
provisionality will fly into fullness.

Ascension Day

Returning where time and space neither exist nor matter,
the uncreated, now fleshed and wounded,
wears our face in heaven, where he prays for us,
waits for us, sends on us again that undivided Love.

Mission ended, mission begun, seamless story
which only humans divide into chapters.

For in Godhead
there is only Love's creative, saving beat.

All our calendars are provisional.
They supply our means of remembrance,
and spur on observance. Eternal truth thus penetrates
our attention and lifts us there.

Christ is risen, ascended, glorified. Alleluia!

Come, Holy Spirit

We can call but not command, invite, but not demand.
Come, Holy Spirit.
He can choose to light our hair or flame the church elsewhere.
Come, Holy Spirit.
He breathes in all that lives, but he himself he gives.
Come, Holy Spirit.
He has no off-limits place yet wears no single face.
Come, Holy Spirit.

Power of God among us.
Come, Holy Spirit.
Love of God within us.
Come, Holy Spirit.
Life of God despite us.
Come, Holy Spirit.
Joy of God to give us.
Come, Holy Spirit.

Wait and pray and wait.
Come, Holy Spirit.
At any time or date.
Come, Holy Spirit.
In him become the place
Come, Holy Spirit.
Where God spreads out his grace.
Come, Holy Spirit.

Trinity Sunday

Nothing happened today.
He was not born nor led out to die.
He did not rise nor ascend on high.
He sent no Spirit upon the Way.

Today he is.
His eternity, not his event, we celebrate.
Awesome to behold and contemplate,
the God who is.

No words can describe his measure,
no metaphor fully explore
the majesty we rightly adore
and earthily treasure.

Holy three times and more,
disclosed to us, withheld from us,
letting us glimpse, saving more for us,
deeper knowledge yet in store.

How can we encapsulate in a sum
the One who cannot be described,
yet who himself has fleshed and scribed,
who was and is and is to come?

At the Gregory Chapel

Christ is in the Aumbry;
seeing the lit flame sets faith ablaze
with all the colours of love.

Here is God in particular,
in a cupboard within all that he has made,
he who cannot be contained.

The elements themselves,
reserved for sick and dying,
are the Gospel in précis,
Christ giving himself
to save and heal us now and always.

He escapes all effort to be constrained,
boxed up, made in our own image.
For this is God, and how can eternity be described?

But there are cracks through heaven's wall, and this is one.
We are permitted an impression,
a glimpse and foretaste of the daylight beyond.

When, eventually, we fall through, it will be into endless light.

Holy City

Jerusalem is where, seeking, I find you,
not in the dusty pathways of sacred history,
nor in the narrow streets clogged with gunmen
and pilgrims on the move,

but where your presence transfigures
wilderness and grace,
and makes a Jerusalem place.

I recall your presence in the comforted yesterdays,
so glad that you were there then.
I saw your face.
But in the daily dying and the going on is
my Jerusalem place.

The Thin Place

You're in love, she said, with the thin place,
and I blushed inside,
and I wished and I tried
to conceal my desire for its solace.

They are sad, she said, are your writings,
and I tried to say
in a casual way
they are therapy, and they are fightings.

    We were talking in the shadow of that old, thin place,
    and I tried to convey how a place is sacrament
    to looking eyes, and disclosure and trace.

Each Visit a Pilgrimage

Each visit a pilgrimage,
and each duty a joy.
I bless Him whom we know here
and His saints at rest in hope.

Each encounter extraordinary
and each moment a gift.
Even the low days and ordinary
yield their efforted fruit.

Each leaving a commissioning
and each leaving a truth,
told in the language of glory
and the metaphors of grace.

Lightning Source UK Ltd.
Milton Keynes UK
UKHW022030170321
380525UK00009B/2293

9 781789 590142